REDNECK SAYIN'S & TERMS

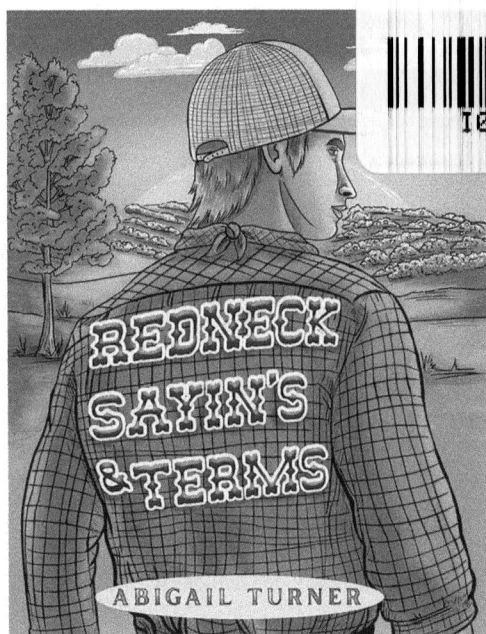

REDNECK
SAYIN'S
&TERMS

ABIGAIL TURNER

Written by: Abigail Turner
Illustrated by: Amy Rottinger

PipStones

PipStones

"Weavers of Tales and Tellers of Truth"

PIPSTONES PUBLISHING
P.O. BOX 4507
FORT WALTON BEACH, FLORIDA 32549
WWW.PIPSTONES.COM

AUTHOR: ABIGAIL TURNER
EDITORS: ABIGAIL TURNER, SHEREE FREDRICKSON, DEBORAH HOFFMAN
ILLUSTRATOR: AMY ROTTINGER- AROTTINGER87@GMAIL.COM

LIBRARY OF CONGRESS CONTROL NUMBER: 2024908459
COPYRIGHT ©2024; PUBLISHED IN 2024

ISBN-13: 979-8-9889427-1-9, PRINT
ISBN-13: 979-8-9889427-2-6, EBOOK

FOR WORLDWIDE DISTRIBUTION
PRINTED IN THE UNITED STATES OF AMERICA

DEDICATION

THIS BOOK IS DEDICATED TO:

My Husband
&
All the Redneck Folks

SPECIAL THANKS TO:

My friends and family for contributing their best Redneck
Sayin's & Terms!

This has been a belly-laughin' journey!

CONTENTS

PREFACE

I moved with my son from Colorado to the South in 2006, a journey that turned into a life I didn't know I would love so much. Alabama is my forever home. I love the people, the quiet, the slower pace, and my house amid a wooded area.

For a while, I had trouble understanding the speech nuances or defining what someone was saying, and there were many things I needed clarified. Now that I can understand the language (most of the time), I suppose I've become one, and I'm good with that! In many ways, though, I'm still a "city girl."

My husband, David, is the inspiration for this book. He was born and raised in our little town called Red Level, Alabama. It's where "Homecomings" aren't just a dance at a local high school in the fall but huge events for schools and churches. Community is essential, and so are the people who live here. I have never seen so many family reunions, and it's an honor if you're invited to one, especially if you're not related.

We live in the Bible Belt— a place I never knew existed. The Red Level community only has 500 plus people, yet there are 13 churches. Yes, you read that right, 13! We also believe in the power of the belt, or at least hand-spankings on the tush of our children when they act up. It's normal to us. Even many schools still have corporal punishment for their students.

With a horse in my front yard, a sawmill, 4 sheds, and acreage, it's quite a different life than my other in Colorado (a postage stamp yard with a fence separating me and my neighbors). Our property is surrounded by family and their land, a concept that is ceasing to exist today. Additionally, my deceased grandmother-in-law owned a community cemetery, and it's still in the family. The cemetery is just a short jaunt around the corner from my house. That is where my husband and I and our children will be eventually buried. It's comforting knowing this, even though we will be with Jesus eternally someday.

Along my Southern journey, I met a wonderful man who I later married. This was one of the best decisions of my life. I love his "reduckness" and the relaxed drawl to his speech. He is the perfect icon for a chivalrous Southern gentleman who's handsome, too! He's a great hunter (with a bow and a gun), a successful businessman, loves his mama, and loves God. A man who is all those things and cares about his family is also something we are losing in our times. We need more Davids in the world!

The way David speaks is what enticed the creation of this book. He's quite a funny guy. One day he said something silly in his "David way," and bingo, there it was— the inspiration for *Redneck Sayin's & Terms*! I decided at that moment that I was going to have some fun writing this book.

Like any other author, I too, have a special writing place. My writing sanctuary is on my front porch church pew. That's right, on an old, wooden church bench! As I script parts of my book, I laugh and giggle, and the birds chirp away while my dog, Zoey, stares intently at me. She's probably thinking, *Mom, you've lost it. Do we need to take you to the vet?*

Well, maybe I have, but it sure was a hoot "losing it!"

I hope you enjoy the words and phrases within. The following stories are based solely on my and my family's experiences and I've certainly had a great time gathering terms from others.

INTRODUCTION

WHO ARE THE REDNECKS?

Rednecks are beautiful, hardworking, and fun people who cherish many of the "old ways" of living, raising their families, working, and speaking. They are made up of those who like the "country" and smooth through life with great sayin's.

Rednecks come in all shapes, sizes, and races. They span vast lands and integrate into all societies, although we consider them originally from the deep South. Some of the terms and words you may read are not from your area, or as we say in the South, "Not from here!"

WHAT TO EXPECT?

Prepare yourself for some good laughs. You may even recognize some of these sayin's and words, and if you don't, well, you're in for a ride!

My focus of this book is to highlight my own memories and experiences of living among the Rednecks who are now my friends and kinfolk. Most definitions are likely outside of a dictionary and are only my and other contributors' views. On a side note... many of the words will contain apostrophes! Be sure to read Chapter 12. This chapter clarifies the misconceptions about Rednecks and explains where this group of people came from, who they were back then, and who they are now.

I encourage you to get a copy of this book for those who have never met a Redneck or may have misunderstood them in the past. If you have "country" friends and kinfolk, *Redneck Sayin's & Terms* is the perfect gift for their grillin' time, mornings sippin' their cowboy coffee, or a good laugh from their front porch swing.

BEWARE...

Ya'll may discover that you are more REDNECK than you thought!

1

VITTLES & GRUB

FOOD
MEALTIME LINGO
COOKIN' STORIES

Mealtime in the South is often a wonderful experience. My mother-in-law, Janice, still cooks up a large meal for Sunday dinner. She invites anyone who's hungry or wants a nibble. It's really an endearing gesture and a time for fellowship. From home-grown veggies to deer steak to the delectable taste of fresh-baked cookies, we leave with full bellies, a peaceable mindset, and certainly ready for a nap.

Sitting at her table is a sure treat. The Bible lies on one end (where she's obviously been doing some studying), and opposite of that is a Christian puzzle. What great moments—eating, talking, and laying those puzzle pieces in the perfect spot. I will forever cherish mealtime at "Mamaw's."

In this chapter, you'll read about our funny and seriously essential food, hunger, and mealtime words! And as we like to say here...

FOOD

BOILED PEANUTS – peanuts that are salted and boiled until the shell and the nut are soft; pronounced as baawld peanuts

> I had never heard of boiled peanuts until I came here, but I've got to say, "They are delicious!" I especially like the spicy Cajun ones.

CATHEAD BISCUITS – humongous, perfectly round, homemade biscuits

CRACKLINS – crispy fried curly pig skin strips

> Be careful not to chip a tooth when eating these. This is why a lot of people cook them in cornbread batter.

TURNIP GREENS – a treat for Sunday meals

COLLARD GREENS – an alternative to turnip greens for Sunday meals

FULL AS A TICK – not hungry anymore

GRITS – a must-eat food for breakfast; sometimes served with butter and cheese on top (cheese grits)

HANKERIN' – a yearning for something specific, usually referring to food

> Don't eat that. It's no good – usually means it's the best food on the table, and someone wants it all for themselves, jokingly (of course).

'JEAT YET? – Did you eat yet?

LIGHT BREAD – basic sliced bread; it can really be wheat or white

MATER GRAVY – tomato gravy

This is undoubtedly not one of my favorites. Honestly, I can barely choke it down. Out here, they love it!

MATER SANDWICH – tomato sandwich; I'd rather have a BLT

MEAL – the long version is called cornmeal

NANNER SANDWICH – banana sandwich; also not a favorite of mine

I'll pass it up every time, but it's one of my husband's quick-treat favorites.

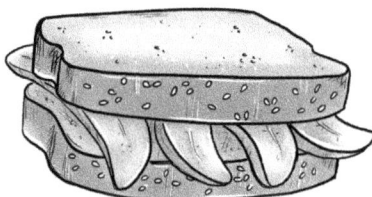

PEAS – these peas are never green (only brown, tan, or yellow); when they refer to English peas, those are the green ones

POT LIQUOR – the juice from your collards or turnips; usually poured over cornbread

POTTED COD (POTTED MEAT) – a hodgepodge of all parts of the animal ground up into a tiny can

Who knows really what's in it? But it's yummy on some saltines.

RHUBARB – a vegetable from the buckwheat family; a delicious and different-tasting vegetable found in a Southern pie (ex: strawberry rhubarb pie)

Rutabaga – a vegetable that is cooked in many Southern pies

Samich – some people refer to a sandwich in this manner

Sounds like two hounds fightin' over a bone – a growling stomach

Sweet tea – a Southerner's favorite drink

> Don't even consider inviting a Southern family over if you ain't got sweet tea!

Vienney sausage – Vienna Sausage; pronounced with a twang

Vittles – yummy food

MEALTIME LINGO

Breakfast – many times served with grits and cathead biscuits

Brunch – doesn't exist

Dinner – middle of the day meal; lunchtime; in other places, it's at night

> Shortly after moving to Alabama, I had an appointment to take my dog to the vet. I delivered my dog and was told to pick him up at dinnertime. I arrived at around 5:30ish to pick him up, and it was closed. I panicked and called the after-hours line posted on the door. As I began telling her my story, she stopped me dead in my tracks and said, "Honey, you're not from around here, are ya?"
>
> Nope, I wasn't, and I learned my lesson quickly...
>
> *DINNER IS IN THE DAYTIME!*

Supper – a meal in the evening

Ice cream – a Sunday outing

> Going out for ice cream (for my husband and me) is still a pleasant little excursion to the local Wages Market Store. We sit on the bench outside, lick on the ice cream while we chat, people-watch, and try not to let the drippings mess up our clothing. It reminds me of the olden

days that were told by my mom when going for ice cream was a special event.

COOKIN' STORIES

Grillin' Time

This one time, I went to the local urgent care and sat near a man with a mouth like a motor. I was there because I had a migraine and was quite nauseous. This man kept loudly talking about all kinds of things... driving, horse manure, large family, four kids, and so on. He was controlling the entire conversation of the sickly waiting room patients.

He began down this road of what he likes to cook up from the wild. Now, I, trying to stifle the puke anyway, am hearing him talk about 'possums. This conversation goes from, "They're really smart creatures," to, "They're best when skinned and fried up on an indoor George Foreman Grill! Man, that's good!"

I never wanted to get back to the patient room so quickly in my life! The thought of being prodded and poked by needles (and I hate needles) was way better than listening to all that!

As I was heading to the back, I hear him say, "Rabbit..." My thoughts were, *Okay, where's the trash can?* At that point, the smell of "cooking" was in my nostrils— a scent I hardly could shake off.

The Little Animal Kind

One of my favorite pastimes was going to the local VFW to play some pool, have a couple of drinks, and schmooze with the veterans. In fact, at one point, I was even a bartender there. I remember a time when a "regular" brought in some stew. It had a distinct smell but one that I could not distinguish. I asked the gentleman what it was, and he jokingly said, "Yankee, why don't you just grab you a bowl? It's meat."

My internal alarm immediately went off! The other guys around the bar began to chuckle. Well, it turned out it was the little animal kind of stew (rabbit). I didn't want to be rude and not eat anything, but I thought running to the bathroom would be worse and leaving my shift early. So, I politely said, "I'm good. I've already eaten. Thank you, though."

They all raved about how good it was, and I happily let them!

Thanksgiving Dinner

Thanksgiving is a time of family, friends, food, and fellowship. Like in most places, we come together, and everyone brings pots and pans full of food. I still need to become more accustomed to the stuffing here, though. To me, stuffing is cooked inside the turkey with spices, butter, breadcrumbs, and other items. Stuffing here is called dressing and is cooked in a pan separately. It usually has some chicken, cornmeal, no breadcrumbs, no spices I've ever used for stuffing, and no ingredients we stuff into a turkey. Yes, it tastes good, but I have difficulty getting my pallet used to it when I'm expecting my traditional stuffing. I'm still hanging on to the phrase "... stuff the turkey."

New Year's Luck

Black-eyed peas, ham, and collard greens are a traditional favorite for the new year. If you cook these up and eat them on New Year's Day, they are supposed to bring you good luck. So, I didn't cook any last year, and now I know why my year was a bit rocky.

2

TICKLED PINK

SILLY SAYIN'S & BAD SAYIN'S

This chapter is about silly things that I have heard over the years. A few of these took me a moment to understand. Sometimes, I've been caught off-guard when I've heard these, but they undoubtedly produced a laugh in the end.

SILLY SAYIN'S

AND WHAT HAVE YA – this is used in place of finishing a description of how to use an object or in place of details within a story

"You take the wrench and begin to turn, and what have ya."

"I was telling that man to go down Hester's Store Road. Then, I told him to turn at the dogleg, and what have ya."

CLEAN YOUR TAIL – scrub that booty

FITS LIKE SOCKS ON A ROOSTER – a sarcastic way of saying it fits perfect; doesn't fit at all

I'D LIKE TO FELL OUT – just about passed out due to shock; got very ill and almost fainted

I RECKON – I suppose

MESSED UP LIKE A SOUP SANDWICH – that person has odd ways of thinking about things

'MON IT! – I'm on it; about to get it done

RUNNIN' AROUND – cheating on your spouse

You see, I was initially from the Midwest. Out there, this term means running errands unless you add the words "On you" at the end of runnin' around.

I'm reminded of a time when my mom and I had many errands in the larger town nearby. After a full day of this, we ended up at my mom's house. My husband came by a bit later and asked me what I had been doing all day. My simple answer was, "Runnin' around."

The shock on his face was priceless as he asked, "Doin' what?" We all burst out laughing when we realized how he took that phrase.

There's no need to explain the rest except that it's been a running joke for a while now with me and David! I am always runnin' around! Haha

SUMMER TEETH – some are teeth, and some aren't

TAIL – your bottom; butt

TAIL TIMBER – a soft-like substance used to wipe your rear end; toilet paper

WONKY OR JANKY – all messed up

WORKS LIKE TITS ON A BOAR – doesn't work at all

Y'ON IT! – you're on it; great job

BAD SAYIN'S

Some of these next terms are watered down a bit, hence the stars. You can spice them up a tad!

AWW SHUCKS – aww shoot

DADGUMMIT OR DADGUM – da** it

DAGNABBIT – da** it

FOR PETE'S SAKE – for goodness sake

OH FOOT – oh man; that's messed up

GOOD GRAVY – good grief

JOHN BROWN – a term for dang it

KNOCK THE DOG-WALKIN' CRAP OUTTA YA – Is there a need to explain this one?

LOOKS LIKE THEY CAN EAT AN APPLE THROUGH A PICKET FENCE – they've got a bad case of bucked teeth

PUT A POP KNOT ON YOUR HEAD – threatening to wallop someone so hard that it creates a tall knot on their head; they may end up needing two tickets to get into the movie theater

SON OF A BISCUIT EATER – S.O.B.E.; a personal favorite of mine

WHAT IN TARNATION? – What is going on?

WHAT IN THE SAM HILL? – What in the hell?

WOBBLE-CODDED BASTARD – a man that is not particularly liked

TO INFINITY & YONDER

3

WHICHAWAY & WHATAWAY

Directions in the South are based on the ultimate in confusion and getting lost! This was and still is my biggest struggle here in Alabama. I'm great at understanding directions and can read almost any map, but the directions people give here have nothing to do with street names or how far you need to travel. That is where I hit a roadblock!

WHICHAWAY

A WAYS OFF <u>OR</u> **A WAYS UP** <u>OR</u> **DOWN** – this really should mean a mile or two, but can end up being more than 30 miles

> "Just drive a ways up that road, and you should be there soon." After about 4 miles, you envision a sign that reads, "The Hills Have Eyes."

BELOW – mainly referring to direction not as in south but rather at the bottom of a hill or before someone's house or place of business

COUNTRY ROADS – these are ere'where and used in regular discussions with directions

> The tricky thing is, most of the time, the signs don't exist or have been changed to another name. And thanks for the song, John Denver; it's become a bedrock for Southern favorites.

DOGLEG – an angle in the road

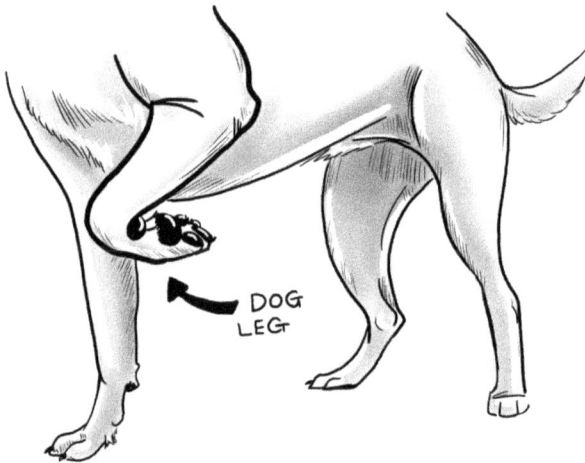

DOG LEG

GETTIN' IN SHORT ROWS NOW! – this term is still used today when talking about completing a task soon

> You see, back when folks would pick cotton by hand, they started with the long rows. As they came to the edges of the field, that is where the short rows were because of the field's shape. So, working the short rows meant that they were almost done.

Monday week – the next Monday coming up but not the Monday of this week; can even use other days of the week to identify the following weeks' time frames

> If it were Sunday and someone says, "We'll be goin' there Monday week," they mean Monday of the following week, not tomorrow. Get it? Got it? Good!

NO DUMP – an actual sign on the side of the road; I reckon it indicates don't put your trash here

> The crazy thing is, I've seen a few of these signs, and sometimes the houses near it are real dumps.

North to get to South:

We have a road named South off a main highway near my house. At one point, it was a community called South. Now, it's just a road. I live North of South. I'm just glad I don't live South of South, but my mom does. She has to drive North to get to South! Can you imagine trying to explain that one to someone not from here?

OAKTREE – a special place by the road that might mark a turn up ahead; many loggers are warned not to cut these when clear-cutting a piece of land

O'ER DERE – over there

OLD OAK TREE – a landmark

OUT CHONDER – it's really a scrunched saying for out yonder, but that would require sounding out the "y" more in the word yonder; out that way

SLOW CHURCH – this appears as a sign by the road indicating that there is a church ahead and that you should slow down

> I believe they should've invested the extra money to add two more words so it would read, "SLOW DOWN, CHURCH AHEAD."
>
> "SLOW CHURCH" is just plain embarrassing.

WHATAWAY

STREET NAMES & SIGNS – they barely exist; many times, they aren't used in giving directions

> Why do we still have these? The signs sometimes look like they're hanging on by a thread (wonky and janky), or like they've been through a hurricane, which could be the case. They might even have a few BB gun divots.

Thisaway & Thataway – anywhere but where they should be; can be meant to describe a drunk person swerving in and out of the lines on a road

> "They were swerving thisaway and thataway."

Turn right there – turning right or left; it doesn't have to be a right turn, just turn at that spot

Yonder – anywhere but here

1. **Over Yonder** – can be left or right according to where you're standing or viewing the front of a structure
2. **Under Yonder** – not entirely sure where this is; I believe it means below an item on the ground or South of an area
3. **Up Yonder** – past a hill, structure, or North of something
4. **Down Yonder** – South in direction or further than where you are currently standing

HELLO & HOWDY-DO

CHIVALRY IS STILL ALIVE!

CHIVALRY IS STILL ALIVE!

One of the most honorable things that a Southern man can do for a lady is open the door for her. On occasion, you might even catch a man tipping their hat to you or calling you, "Ma'am." These are gestures that a lot of Southern gentlemen still do.

Let me break it down using a specific episode of "Gomer Pile." The female Lieutenant is offended because Gomer keeps tipping his hat to her and calling her Ma'am instead of saluting and addressing her as Lieutenant. She makes the biggest deal out of it and makes him do extra duties to suffice her "lieutenant stature."

To make a long story short, the Lieutenant finally concludes that Gomer is just a Southern gentleman and has a sweet way about him with a different kind of respect for women. It's something that she realizes was ingrained in him from a young age and wasn't going to change. Many "redneck men" are embedded with those same values. It's about honoring a lady with simple gestures and courtesies.

COWBOYS & COWGIRLS (KIDS) – kids that are little rodeo stars are loved by the crowd

They are the real heroes at the rodeos, riding those sheep and smaller bulls and competing in poles and barrels on their little ponies. It takes some guts to do that! There are even young boys who ride the smaller bulls or buckin' broncos.

GOOD PEOPLE – a phrase used when the entire family is liked by the community

HONKING – a car honk means, "Hello! I know you!"

HORSE SENSE – common sense

LIKE TWO PEAS IN A POD (POT) – get along well; similar in many ways; some people change the word pod to pot

LIL' BIT – a small person

MA'AM – all children must refer to women in this manner; it is totally unacceptable to say anything else

> My son kept getting into trouble after his first days in school here because he couldn't get used to calling the teacher Ma'am. I had to explain to her that the term, "Ma'am," was not used where I was from, but that we would work with him on it. After time, my son learned the "Ma'am" lingo and his teacher was happy as a Lark.

MIGHTY PURTY – if you receive this compliment, you look pretty beautiful

> I tried my best to look beautiful on my husband and my first date. I had a floral yellow and green dress on, some lovely dress sandals, and hair long and flowing. When he picked me up and we got in the car, what he said to me was something I will never forget, and one of the sweetest things I had ever heard a Southern gentleman say. David peered into my eyes, gave me a little side smile, and tenderly said, "You sure look mighty purty, Miss Abby." I almost started crying. Finally, a sweet man with some manners. I felt like a real lady. David had a certain softness in his demeanor, yet he was a completely manly man. And... as the story goes, I was hooked, and we eventually got married.

NO BIGGER THAN A MINUTE – a tiny person; petite

> This is certainly not a term I am accustomed to. I am indeed "bigger than a minute," not fat, just "bigger than a minute." But that reminds me of a time when my father-in-law had passed away. On the church obituary, my name was printed as Abigal. I took that as a A Big Gal! Even though the funeral proceedings weren't by any means funny, I just knew that my father-in-law would've gotten a kick out of that— Papaw had a good sense of humor! My husband, niece, and I

laughed together, envisioning how Papaw would've chuckled about that.

PRETTIER THAN A SPECKLED PUPPY UNDER A RED WAGON – if you get this compliment, you are anywhere between an 8 and a 10

PUNKIN' – a sweet term used to describe a nice young person

SIT A SPELL – stay a while

> Someone may tell you this when you come to their house to visit. If they don't, you might as well get on down the road.

SPORT – a rambunctious kid

SPORT MODEL – a cute but sassy little girl

SOUTHERN WAVE – only requires one index finger up from the steering wheel, not a full hand wave or a California-style wave (with the middle finger up, you know, the bird)

When a friend from Colorado came to visit, she and I were sitting on my parents' long wrap-around porch. The few cars that drove by gave us an Alabama wave. She asked me why all the people driving by were flipping us off. I proudly said, "They're waving at us. It's just something we are not used to, Jan." I think she was surprised at the common courtesies held as a standard here. I was, too.

TAKE A GANDER – you try it; you look at it and figure it out

Y'ALL COME BACK NOW, YA HEAR? – they are kindly telling you that you and your family are accepted back some time; that you probably are "good people"

Y'ALL KIN? – are you family-related

I find out almost daily that I have a larger extended family from David's side of the tree. My response is usually something like, "What? We're related to them, too?"

5

THE GREATER OUTDOORS

COUNTRY & CRITTERS

My first trip to my parent's house in Red Level was wild! I was caught in a rainstorm between Fort Walton Beach, Florida, and just past the Alabama line. I had never been in a rainstorm like this. It was intense, and I kept dodging "things" on the road. It was hard to figure out what these things were as it was difficult to see. Well, come to find out, it was animals. In the South, this is what we call roadkill! I had never seen so many dead animals on one trek! It's almost like it rained cats and dogs, and of course, other creatures too!

COUNTRY & CRITTERS

A BLIND SQUIRREL CAN FIND A NUT EVERY NOW AND THEN – this sayin' is aimed at a person who finally figured out something simple

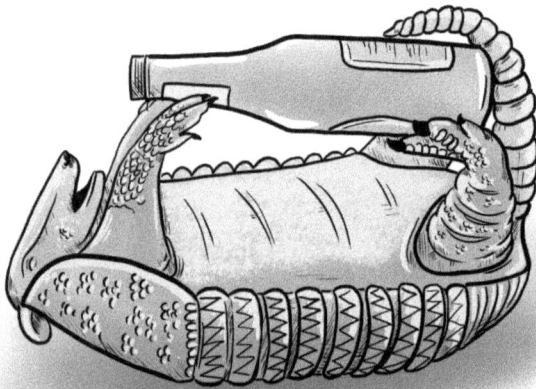

ARMADILLER – armadillo

Highway 55 is the road I call the Indy 55. It's where we fight the beachgoer traffic and everyone traveling for the holidays. Trust me, it can be a scary trek! Well, back in 2007, I spotted a little animal on the side of the 55, the thing we call an armadiller. I couldn't help it, but I started busting out laughing. This little guy was lying on his back, and in his paws was a beer bottle. He was just lying there soaking up the sun but was dead as a doornail. Right then and there, I wasn't sure if I was the one with the sick humor or the person who played that prank, but it sure was funny!

BRANCH – a small creek that runs through the woods (a term usually used in the South)

CRICK – creek; a term usually used in the Midwest (requires some redneckness)

FOOD PLOTS – plats of land that are prepared for the deer and other wildlife to feed off

> This phrase threw me for a loop. I honestly thought it was a garden where I would soon gather veggies and cook them in my cast-iron skillet (a must-have pan in the South). Well, I was wrong about these plats of land. They're actually worked on each evening starting in September with the plowing, preparing, and planting. Then, the waiting process begins. The deer begin to feel comfortable returning day after day to feed off this area until, one day during hunting season, they "meet the Maker." They are shot and skinned for an ultimate freezer or pan-fried experience. They sometimes make a beautiful trophy for the wall.

GOPHER – not an actual gopher, but really a land tortoise

HOTTER THAN THE DEVIL'S TOENAILS! – that sure is hot; this is what it feels like during the summertime in the South

IT'S LIKE A COW PISSIN' ON A FLAT ROCK OUT THERE! – raining extremely hard

NOODLING – when you stand in lake water and use your arm to catch catfish; your arm may end up in the mouth of a catfish

POLECAT – skunk; a bad person

STRAY – an animal that you know is not yours and roams around the neighborhood, coming back again and again until you finally take it in and give it a name

THE BOTTOM FELL OUT – pouring rain and not letting up

WHITE CRANE – a White Crane

In the South, they have some odd names for creatures. Occasionally, someone will ask, "What do you call that?" Well, my dad made this mistake, knowing the honest answer already. He asked my husband, "What do you call that white bird that follows the cows? It looks like a Crane."

David answers, "A White Crane!" An explosion of laughter followed.

It goes to show that some things appear to be normal and others not.

ZERO-TURN MOWER – a must for any mowing job

It took me a while to get used to the heat and humidity in the South. My almost first heat stroke occurred shortly after moving while I was hand-mowing the lawn in the middle of August. That ended my mowing excursions quickly! Heat plus humidity plus bugs was not my thing!

On the tails of this, someone told me I needed a Zero-Turn Mower... I quickly replied, "Okay!" I knew I had to get one if I was going to survive! I'm happy to say that my husband faithfully mows our lawn. Thank God for David and the riding lawnmower. We need to upgrade to a Zero-Turn, but David is a tough guy! He calls ours a 4-acre turn mower!

6

ERE'WHERE & ERE'ONE

NECK OF THE WOODS

KINFOLK

WHAT IN THE WORLD?

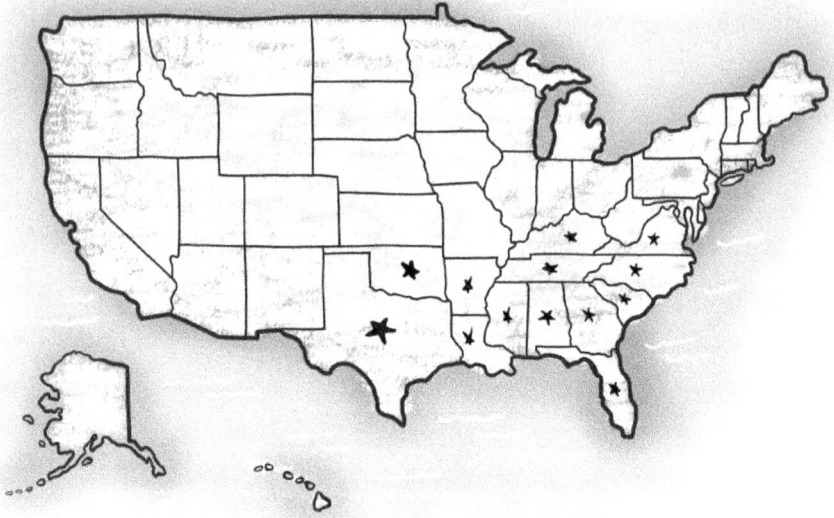

NECK OF THE WOODS

BEER JOINTS – small bars with pool tables and steady staff; places that sometimes break out into a bar fight

HONKY TONKS – bars with old-style country bands playing

JUKE JOINTS – bars with dancing and music; also called a bar

WALMART – the local one-stop old friend shop

Walmart is a meeting place where you run into old friends you haven't seen in a while and talk amongst the isles for 5-15 minutes.

I figured out pretty quickly that Walmart was not just a store but a meeting place. It's where you go when you're bored and might have some shopping to execute.

My husband knows everyone. Our trips to Walmart are lengthy. I'm not a slow shopper, so this is still difficult for me to handle. I learned quickly to introduce myself because David can't remember everyone's names. It's probably because he knows everyone! That's a lot of names to keep up with.

KINFOLK

CHITLINS – sometimes children can be called chitlins; pig intestines

Many folks still cook these and serve chitlins (not the children kind) as a specialty item at BBQs.

GRANDMA & GRANDPA – those names don't exist

Alternative Grandma & Grandpa names: Memaw, Pepaw, Mamaw, Papaw, Big Mama, Big Daddy, Grandpop, Grandaddy, Pop-Pop, Pops, Granny, Grampappy, and even G-G. You may even have others to add to this list.

Your Family Name List:

\------------------------

\------------------------

\------------------------

\------------------------

HUSBAND – some wives refer to them as their old man; better half

I'VE BEEN KNOWIN' THEM – proud of having known that person for a long time OR a warning to you about them *because* they've known them for a long time

I'VE BEEN STUDYIN' ON THEM – watching a person but not usually in a creepy way, just trying to figure them out; observing a person's character

KIN OR KINFOLK – family relatives

MOM & DAD – Mother, Daddy, Pops, Mama

MOMINEM – mom and them

SON – anyone under 50 can be referred to as son, even by someone their own age

WIFE – old lady; ball and chain; better half; main squeeze

These are much older terms. People have now become more civilized referring to their spouses unless they want a frying pan across the forehead.

WHAT'S YOUR LAST NAME? – a critical question when meeting someone for the first time; the answer defines a status; "I know everyone around."

YOUNGIN' – a child

WHAT IN THE WORLD?

ACCENT – anyone who doesn't have a southern drawl has an accent

I have been told "umpteen" times that I have an accent. I laugh because, to me, everyone here has an accent.

COLDER THAN A WITCH'S TITTY IN ALASKA – extreme cold

COLDER THAN A WELL-DIGGER'S A** IN IDAHO – also extreme cold

DEEWALL DITTY – a far-off place, maybe further than the South

Ere'body – everybody

Ere'one – everyone

Ere'where – everywhere

Flora-Bama – a popular place in between the Alabama and Florida line; don't blink, or you'll pass right through it; if you stop, be prepared to party

L.A. – Lower Alabama

I love it when people ask where I live, and my answer usually confuses them a bit when I tell them L.A.

Not from here – someone who takes a long time to be accepted by the general population in the community

YANKEE – anyone not from the South, no matter where they previously lived, is called a Yankee

> When I worked at the VFW, everyone called me a Yankee, even though I had moved from the Midwest. That didn't matter to them. I wasn't from here; therefore, I was a Yankee. If someone here calls you that, don't think they are trying to fight ya. They probably like you and feel comfortable teasing you.

WHO OPENED THE GATE? – this is usually asked when there is a constant stream of cars and you can't pull out into the intersection

7

WHO'S WHO

THE GOOD
THE BAD
THE UGLY

THE GOOD

THE BAD!

THE UGLY

There are those who always try to do good. And those who successfully do bad. But, why is it that some people just like to be ugly? Now, I know what you're thinking, but hold your horses! Being ugly has a whole different meaning to a Redneck.

THE GOOD

AH'IGHT – alright

BE THERE IN TWO SHAKES OF A STICK – be there soon

FINER THAN FROG'S HAIR SPLIT 5 WAYS – doing great

Fixin' to – going to; also said as fickin' to or fin-na

Garonteed or I Garontee it – guaranteed

> Do you remember Justin, the Cajun Cook? Many men around here still use his ways of saying a few things. Bless his heart.

Gooduns – good ones

Gussied up – all dressed up

Holler atcha later – call ya later; talk to ya later

Homecoming – Class Of... :

> In the South, Homecoming is a special event that happens once a year. Not only does the school vote on kings and queens like in other places, but many of the decades of classmates get together. Often, they create a parade float, have cookouts, and schmooze with their old friends. You see, I came from a class size of almost 500 students, but in small towns, you may have 15-40 classmates. So, ere'one knows ere'body and their personal business too. They've kept good relationships throughout the years and tried their best to get along. It's neat to see this and gives you a sense of what community is.

Homecoming – Bring Us Home, Lord:

> Homecomings are also for the churches on one designated day within the year. All the older members are invited, and new and current members (if the church still has services). The church ladies will go in and clean, and the men will set up tables and organize the furniture. The church invites a speaker or past preacher to give it a good Jesus heave-ho. They have "a singin'," and then all the churchgoers gather for a feast. Most of this food is homemade by all the attendants. Talk about some great and unique recipes, and you leave feeling full as a tick. In Colorado, we would have called the eating part of this event a church potluck. Here, it's called a spread.

That can mean a couple things... 1. A spread on the table, and 2. A spread around your waste.

I reckon – I suppose; I plan on doing that; I think that they...

Peckin' along – consistently working or doing things

Shinin' like a diamond in a goat's butt – looking cleaned up and pretty

Shug – a sweet way of addressing a younger person

Twice two – I'm positive that will work

THE BAD

Are you mad with me? <u>or</u> **Are you mad with him?** – there is definitely something wrong, and someone is about to find out what

BLEEDIN' LIKE A STUCK HOG – blood ere'where

CATTYWAMPUS – something that is not straight

GET YOUR GOAT – someone trying to irritate you

> This phrase was used way back in the day when goats were paired
> with a racehorse to keep them calm. When someone wanted to upset
> the racehorse and make it perform poorly, they would take their goat,
> hoping the horse would lose the race.

HE CAN'T BEAT HIS WAY OUT OF A WET PAPER BAG – a weakling in
strength and possibly even weak in brain power

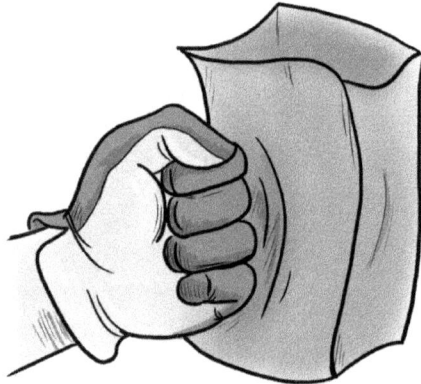

I'M GOIN' TO THE HOUSE! – someone who is really ticked off and
going to their only place of refuge (their home)

I'M GONNA SNATCH A KINK IN HIS TAIL! – gonna kick his butt; put
him on a straight path

JOKER – someone who's less than a good person

MASH IT – not referring to potatoes, but instead pressing with force on
any button that could easily break

My stent working at Walmart gave me a trove of much-needed Alabama knowledge. I worked with a lady who was, let's say, COUNTRY! This lady was a trip! I used to run the "walkie-stacker" in the back warehouse, and sometimes the controller would get stuck. My friend hollered at me to mash the button. I hollered back, "Well, what do you want me to do, break it?" She ran over and grabbed that thing and started mashing the buttons so hard, and I was sure it would break, but it didn't. I decided right there that I'd stick to mashing taters.

OFF-KILTER – either referring to a person that is messed up in the head or an object that is not relatively straight

OUTLAWS – those that have had serious run-ins with the law

Since my husband knows everyone, the stories he has told me would blow your mind about the so-called "outlaws" in our area. You never know exactly who you're talking to and what they have done. The conversation sometimes goes like this, "See that guy over there, he stabbed a man back in the 90's" OR "That guy you just met used to take his car and outrun the police and would spin donuts in the dirt around the cop cars."

PLOW A MULE TO DEATH – if you're told that you could plow a mule to death, you walk way too fast, slow down

I'm a fast walker. Where I'm from, you had to hurry in that fast-paced life. Most times now, I'm halfway across the parking lot before I realize I've just left David in the dust. I can't help it, but I'm working on learning to slow down and breathe in the fresh air. He always says, "Abby, you could plow a mule to death!"

STUMP-SET – something that has been knocked out of alignment

"That looks like it's been stump-set."

This term comes from plowing in a field where there were stumps. Sometimes, the plow would hit one, and the plow would end up bent. It had been stump-set. Another way of stump-setting is when you get mad at an object, put it on a stump, and smash it with a hammer! Well, that's what I've been told. Haha!

SYRUP SOPPIN' SAP SUCKER – this is said about people they don't like

THAT THING COULDN'T PULL A GREASY STRING OUT OF A HOG'S BUTT – when a tool or a vehicle is too weak to do its job

TIGHTER THAN A DUCK'S BUTT – someone who is extremely tight with their money

THE UGLY

BLESS YOUR HEART – this is almost a tradition for women from the South to say this. It may mean you feel sorry for someone OR, "Wow, too bad they don't have any brains."

If someone is saying this to you, tread lightly; they may be insulting you, or they may feel bad for you.

GAG A MAGGOT – smells horrifically terrible

HE COULD MAKE A FREIGHT TRAIN TAKE A DIRT ROAD – hideous-looking guy

HEFFER – a term used to describe a woman you don't like

ILL – mad and grumpy

ILL BUTT – mad and grumpy

IN THE BED – they are sleeping because they are "ill" or absolutely exhausted

MAKE A BUZZARD PUKE – nasty smells

NUTTIER THAN A FRUITCAKE – crazy person

PUNY – feeling and looking somewhat sickly

SHE'S A MESS – she's got a lot of problems; it may also mean they are always getting into something or have a good sense of humor

SHE'S GOT A BUTT LIKE A PLOW MULE – big and wide butt; only those that have plowed a field with a mule can know the fullness of this phrase, but we all can use our imagination

SWITCH –a device used to tune the behind of a child; often a short, thin stick

> If you see a mama with her car stopped and she's heading toward the grassy area, she's probably not peeing or having car trouble. She may be cuttin' that switch. There must be kid trouble.

THEY'RE JUST A TAD OFF – a little weird

WAIT A COTTON-PICKIN' MINUTE – someone who needs more explanation from what they just witnessed

YOU'RE BEING UGLY – acting in a mean way

8

FULL
CIRCLE

LIVIN'
DYIN'
LIFE IN THE SLOW LANE
TOUCHDOWN

LIVIN'

AMEN, BROTHER BEN – no matter who you're talking to, they could be Ben if they are in agreeance with you

EASE ON BACK TO THE HOUSE – getting ready to go home

GET ON OR GO ON – being told to go to your own house or wherever you came from

> If an individual tells you this, you might want to "ease on out." They obviously don't want you there.

GREW UP HARD – grew up poor and without many extra amenities

> Many people in my community "grew up hard." The money never came easy, and most worked in the fields or on a farm. Times were tough, but they never knew any different. It was normal to them. The things that mattered were God, family, home, and work. I admire them

greatly for this. If a majority of people would've grown up hard, they would be a lot more appreciative of life.

GREW UP IN A HOLLER – grew up in a shack or run-down place; sometimes these places were amid the woods

HOME CHURCH – the church that you and your family usually go to

HANGIN' IN THERE LIKE A LOOSE TOOTH – a resilient person; an object that won't let go

HANGIN' ON LIKE A HAIR IN BISCUIT – barely hanging on to life itself

I'VE BEEN COVERED UP – super busy

LISTEN – this means you won't talk while they tell the longest story they've got in their head and blow it up to be more than it is

LISTEN HERE (PRONOUNCED AS LISTEN HEEYA WITH NO R) – they want you to listen while they tell a story about someone they're "mad with," OR they are about to tell jokes on someone

LIVIN' ON HIGH COTTON – wealthy people; generational wealth

SIT A SPELL – stay a while

SNATCH A TEAR OUTTA YA – make you cry

TAKE A BATH – usually means to take a shower and not usually a bath for adults

UP IN THERE – someone can be pointing out where people or animals are hanging out

"Did you see all those Rednecks up in there?"

DYIN'

GO ON – die and go to heaven

COME TO JESUS MEETIN' – the person that is saying this is upset about something and about to set you straight, or you might meet Jesus tonight

GO REST HIGH – a perfect song for southern funerals; usually performed in the Southern Gospel style

Restaurant Life

I couldn't figure out what was happening for the longest time when my husband and I would go to a restaurant and the hostess would seat us. David would usually want to sit at a different table than she originally led us to. He's a simple man and not snooty, so it never made sense. Finally, I asked him, "David, why is it that every time we are at a restaurant being seated, you want to sit somewhere else?"

And there it was... the simple answer, "I like to be able to see the front door and the exits."

Okay, that blew my mind. So, after all that wondering, it was a protective reaction. David was going to be ready in case anything happened in that restaurant. I think about it now, and that's precisely him – ready for anything. He hunts not because he likes to kill game but because it prepares us for the future. In fact, he's told me before that if we had never been married, he might have just gone to "live off the land." It all makes sense, considering his heroes are Davey Crockett and Daniel Boone. It seems as though I have my own Davey Crockett at home.

LIFE IN THE SLOW LANE

1. Be patient on country roads. It's highly likely you will get behind a gigantic tractor that takes up both lanes.

2. Be prepared to stop on the side of the road and grab a couple pieces of cotton for your visiting friends.

3. Hold your horses when following the elderly. You might want to avoid passing them; it can be dangerous. Swerving can often be their forte.

TOUCHDOWN

College football is primary in the South. I had a student who asked me what football team I supported. Being from Colorado, I said, "The Broncos."

Not thinking before she spoke, she spewed, "The Broncos stink! I go for Alabama!"

I started explaining that the Broncos were a pro team, and then I stopped dead in my tracks. I didn't want to hurt her feelings, so I blurted out, "Roll Tide!"

She smiled and assuredly replied, "See, we do have something in common, Miss Turner."

'Nuff said there.

The Iron Bowl

A Southern Clash of the Titans. It's a huge event after Thanksgiving when two teams fight to the death over the football, and everyone screams and shouts... "Roll Tide!!!!" or "War Eagle!!!!" You're either crimson and white or orange and blue. There are no colors in between, and if you're not invited to watch this battle at a local house, you're probably not a true fan of either team!

I'm still confused about the whole mascot thing with these two teams. You see, the University of Alabama has an elephant but nothing that would make you tie it to the words, "Roll Tide!" Maybe they could at least call the elephant Rolland. On the other hand, Auburn University's mascot is a tiger, yet they yell, "War Eagle!"

Well, I guess it's just another one of those redneck things. I suppose someone will explain it to me one day, but I hope they say it with a thick accent so I can take in the whole experience.

9

THE
CAST-IRON POT

HODGEPODGE

HODGEPODGE

ALL GIVED OUT – worn out

BIGUN – big one

BUGGY – a shopping cart or a horse carriage

I was born in Nebraska, a place where a buggy is a horse carriage. Not here— a buggy is a shopping cart in these parts. I still can't get used to calling it that. When I worked at Wal-Mart, an associate came over the loudspeaker and asked any available employees to get buggies. I stood there for a moment, thinking, *get what?* Then my "country friend" nudged me and said, "Let's go." I had no idea what I was about to get into, but as it turns out, I never wanted to get those "buggies" again. I think I ran over my foot about 10 times and pinched several fingers that day. Unfortunately, I *did* have to perform this task many times. I have a lot of compassion for the "buggy getters." "Bless their hearts," is all I can say.

BUSY A BARK – getting super cold

CARRY YA THERE – drive you there

CAST-IRON POT OR PAN – necessary for making the best cornbread, cat-head biscuits, and often, a casserole

CHUNK THAT TO ME – throw it to me

COME ALONG – a trailer used to haul equipment

CRANK IT – start your car or other engine

CUT THAT OFF – turn it off as in a light off or an engine off

CUT THAT ON – turn it on as in a light on or an engine on

DADGUM THING – dang old thing

ERE'TING – everything

HIGH ON THE HOG – people who are wealthy, or at least pretend they are

HOBO – a large garbage can

> I always knew a hobo to be a homeless person who traveled from place to place by train.

IF'N – short for "if and when"

> "If'n I get my grocery shoppin' done on time, I'll come over."

I'MONA – I'm gonna; I'm going to

MOONSHINE – a high-proof liquor that is usually made in the "backwoods" and is often sold illegally

Piggies – toes

Push water – gasoline

Road-grade lyme – a type of Lyme rock used to pave many a road in these here parts

> My dad mistakenly asked a local guy what kind of rock to use for his driveway. This man went on and on and on and on about the wonderful characteristics of road-grade lyme. My dad finally looked at my husband and said, "If he mentions road-grade lyme one more time..." As the story goes, my dad did end up rocking his driveway with road-grade lyme. I often wonder if the gentleman raving about the product should've worked for a company that produced it. He'd probably be the CEO by now.
>
> Sometimes, we tend to get a little carried away around here, especially if it's something we love.

Rurnt it – ruined it; sometimes it means someone burned the food

Toboggan or Suggan – a warm cloth hat for the head

The actual definition of a toboggan – a long, flat-bottomed light sled usually made of thin boards curved up at one end with usually low handrails at the sides

The actual definition of a suggan – a coverlet for a horse's back used instead of a saddle

We call a suggan a beanie where I was from.

TOTE IT – to carry something

TUMPED OVER – turned over

WRASSLERS – wrestlers

Y'ONTO – Do you want to?

10

SHOOT LOW, SHERIFF! HE'S RIDIN' A SHETLAND!

FOR THE LOVE OF THE GAME

You got game? Well, most folks around here do! They display it on their walls, sheds, as rugs, decals on their vehicles, on their clothing and accessories, and even on baby blankets. We love the thrill of the chase and that one chance to see the game you've been waiting for!

FOR THE LOVE OF THE GAME

Tweet, Tweet

My husband and I were at my parent's house visiting and chalking up conversation. My mom mentions all the robins in the yard and how pretty they are.

David pipes up and says, "Them are good eatin'!" The shock hit our faces, and all of us burst out laughing. The thought of this cute and innocent bird, filleted at the stake, didn't strike our appetite as anything we would want to try.

Now, think about this, David does go on a dove shoot once a year. Before he leaves on his trip, I make sure to tell him, "Give the ones you get to the other guys." He and I have an understanding. I stick to store-bought food, home-grown veggies, and portions of local livestock, or the deer meat he brings home.

If times got tough, though, I'd be out there helping cook these little, precious things up! I'm not that much of a city girl.

Gobble, Gobble

The local VFW puts on a Turkey shoot a couple of times per year. My first encounter with this event was at this particular VFW when I worked there. I really thought the participants would gather and shoot turkeys (which might not be an uncommon practice in the South).

But no, they actually bet on the prizes (slabs of meat, blocks of cheese, pork links, money, etc.). They stood in a horizontal line and shot at targets, waiting to see who came the closest to the center of the X. Whew! I was glad to see this. I was happy to know I wouldn't be skinning up some gobbler at the "festival of turkey trot trot!" What a fun gathering with no de-feathering!

An Old-Timey Turkey Shoot

With that story in mind, I thought I'd give you some background on an original Turkey Shoot. So, the object was to win a turkey from the pen. No, they weren't shooting these turkeys on-site. They would pay money to shoot at a target and see who came closest, just like they do today. That either would win the turkey of their choice from the pen or a 1/5 of moonshine. Eventually, that turkey probably became part of their Thanksgiving feast or, at least, their very own vocal yard dog. The moonshine became their favorite party drink.

Ruff, Ruff

The term dog hunting definitely did not sit well with me! Come to find out, it's not the hunt *of* dogs but rather *with* dogs. You see, it's a large gathering of hunters, of course, wearing their bright orange hats and camo disguises with walkie-talkies in their hands and guns on their sides.

These men and women arrange themselves amongst the woods as the dogs get the deer up and moving, toward the hunters' ultimate kill zone.

I honestly can barely understand David's vocabulary when he comes home from a dog hunt. Most of the time, I know who he's been dog-hunting with, depending on the thick drawl coming out of his mouth.

Coon On A Log

A long time ago, they used to play a game called Coon on a Log. This was a competition in which each hunter would choose their best coon-dog. Then, the dog would wait at the water's edge until prompted to jump into the water. In the middle of the stream or pond was a large log with a raccoon in a cage on top of it. Tied to the log was a long rope held by a man on the other side of the waterway. He would pull on the rope until the raccoon reached his side.

Meanwhile, the dog would attempt to catch the cage. The fastest and most successful dog won! Can you believe that this game is still played in some places?

11

NUMBER 2

THE 2ND AMENDMENT

THE 2ND AMENDMENT

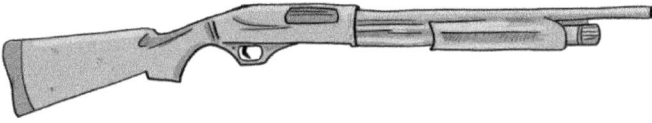

If you want to make a Redneck ticked off faster than stirring up a hornet's nest, or you want a boot stuck up your butt, then just mention taking away our 2nd Amendment right. Even whisperings of banning certain guns will not make for a pretty conversation among my people.

The consensus is this, "Leave us and our guns alone!"

You see, Southerners know from history that a people without protection can be subject to be overthrown. It is the people who own these United States, not the government. It is our money that creates government jobs and provides for the people. This is something that many seem to forget. Some Americans believe the government pays for welfare, medical benefits, and jobs. The government produces nothing; we do it all with our hard-earned pennies. They spend, and we provide.

We want to keep our right to protect ourselves and our way of life from the government, if necessary, and from renegades. We also believe that the "old ways" of providing food for our family are essential for future survival. It's called hunting, plain and simple, and we should be able to have the proper weapons to hunt. We also occasionally enjoy the practice of shooting at a target for recreation.

I like to think of myself as a decent archer. Am I a professional? Not by any means, but I enjoy the sport of archery. I could hunt if necessary, but as of now, I don't have the gumption nor the desire to kill an animal myself.

Am I an anarchist? Absolutely not! I believe in and support law and order one hundred percent. I also think that some regulation is necessary. What I don't like is the overreaching control from those in Washington, D.C., and even our own state governments.

Here's a prime example of what the government and others continually try to control in our 2nd Amendment: "... <u>shall not be infringed</u>." In the 2nd Amendment, this line is clear. The government and individuals do not have the right to interfere in our constitutional right to bear and keep arms.

THE 2ND AMENDMENT:

"A well-regulated Militia [that's us], being necessary to the security of a free State, the right to keep and bear Arms, <u>shall not be infringed</u>."

VICTORY:

I have a relative who has family that lives in England. Her family was saying that they could not believe how we can have guns here. In fact, they are entirely against us bearing arms.

My thoughts are this... *Well, Englanders, we fought in a war called the Revolutionary War. In that, we defended our right to be free. We became an independent nation from the tyranny and overreaching control of guess who... Yes, England, you. With the blood that was shed by our brave militia and the decisions of our leaders, we are a free United States today. Do you remember Paul Revere, riding his horse through the streets of Boston, Massachusetts, hollering, "The British are coming!"? Yep, that would be your people attacking us. So, I might tell you, "Thanks." You pushed us into a corner, and we became victorious.*

Our 2nd Amendment right is in our Constitution because our forefathers were not about to let a government control us again, including our own. We, the people, have the right to defend our families and our freedoms.

I suggest you and other nations listen to the words in our "Star Spangled Banner," a song scripted amid the bombs bursting during the War of 1812 (another war with Great Britain). This is the cherished composition of our country's principles! We are the... "Land of the free and the home of the brave."

Leave us and our guns alone!

12

HISTORY

BAMA FACTS
REDNECKS THEN & NOW

BAMA FACTS

1. Alabama is called Alabama the Beautiful for a reason. Does that surprise you? You know you've arrived in Alabama when you see the lush greenery, spreading waterways, and its little fishing nooks.

2. The Yellowhammer is the state bird.

3. The state tree is the Longleaf Pine. This tree was used to make many coffee tables and even homes.

4. There are 450 species of fish found in Alabama. It is home to more fish than any other state in North America.

5. Alabama has more streams and rivers than any other state.

REDNECKS THEN & NOW

There are many misconstrued messages about how the term Redneck evolved. Although I don't claim to be a historian of this term, I have done a bit of research to help clarify a few things. You may have heard some of the associations of the name Redneck, like Reds, Appalachians, and Hillbillies. These titles aren't far from the depth of the word Redneck, yet their origins are widespread throughout the South and make up a conglomeration of people from various states. In this chapter, I break down these terms and their meanings.

West Virginia the Coal-Rich State:
The names Red and Red Neck

Between 1912 and 1919, coal was a massive industry for America, as it was necessary for fighting World War I. West Virginia was one of the leading mining states.

At that time, there was an increase in the presence of a strong coal miner's union in that state. There were those who didn't want to be part of the union and those who did. The promise of financial security, continuation of work, and safety was appealing to the union workers, which made them loyal to that stability. By 1920, the miners began to show this loyalty by wearing red bandanas around their necks, and they went on strike in solidarity for their rights. They were labeled as Red Necks or Reds.

Many people throughout history have claimed that these Reds were communists. However, it has been proven through specific accounts that the Union brought people together to work toward common goals: to earn a living wage for their families, provide America with as much coal as it needed, and work in a safer environment. The idea was to unite immigrants, blacks, and whites into one brotherhood of equal pay and human rights.

In an attempt to prevent unionization, the federal, state, and county governments, influenced by wealthy railroad and coal company bosses began jailing and mistreating the leaders of its cause. The pot had been stirred, and the workers weren't going to see this happen. That's when things came to a head!

August 1921:
Battle at Blair Mountain

Armed coal miners marched, rode trains, and drove vehicles from Kanawha Valley, collecting more miners along the way until finally reaching Blair Mountain. Many were said to be World War I veterans, and knew how to form, prepare, and strategize their efforts. They were a commoners' marching militia.

As the battle between miners and the governments erupted, the ridges of Blair Mountain became a war zone. President Warren G. Harding ended this conflict by sending an aircraft bomber squadron and 2,500 troops to engage the Reds. Many of the World War veterans did not want to fire on the federal government's military. It is unknown how many people died in this battle; to say a number is only speculation. Several hundred people were charged with various crimes, from murder to treason. This famous battle and other state's coal battles are known as the Mine Wars.

Men of Old and the Wild:
The names Appalachian and Hillbilly

The people of the mountains and hills in states such as West Virginia, Virginia, Kentucky, Tennessee, and Alabama lived off the land and strived to provide food for their tables. These people were considered Appalachians. They were hunters, gardeners, weavers, and even moonshiners.

Eventually, many men joined the coal mining or logging industries for financial stability. But they never let go of their roots. Family continued to be a priority, as did their traditions and "ways of old." Common sense and a grasp on survival were more important to them than book sense. That is why others refer to them as backwoods Hillbillies. They try to paint them with an uneducated brush. However, isn't it true that what we have learned comes from our roots and lessons from these "men of old?" In my opinion, they helped shape the South. All the while, the government tried to infringe on their way of life through taxation, land takeovers, and demands to become urbanized.

Country Folk:
The Southerners

The states with stars on the map from Chapter 6 are the states with the highest populations of this group (or at least that's what my horse sense says). We are the South! We are a God-fearing, family-oriented, land-owning, root-lovin', country-ridin', assortment of people. Independence and freedom is a large factor to a Southerner's way of life.

Occasionally, we like to take a nice dirt road ride on the 4-wheeler or do a bit of mud-bogging. We may even head over to the local pond and throw in a pole. It's not uncommon for you to pull up to someone's house and see a rooster running around their yard. We live a simplistic life and enjoy even the small things that God has provided for us.

Rodeos are packed-out events, and so are our lakes in the heat of summer— which, by the way, is HOT and HUMID between June and August! But there is nothing like sitting on a front porch swing on a perfect evening in early spring. Our winters aren't too bad either. That's why we have "snowbirds," the retired people from the Northern states who stay for wintertime.

So, I suppose this defines how simply Redneck we are.

Rednecks Today:
The Melting Pot

As I've explained, Appalachians, Hillbillies, Reds, and Red Necks can be considered part of the term Redneck.

Throughout our Appalachian and Southern states, our primary industries are coal mining, logging, cotton, tobacco, and seafood. A few of our technological growing industries are automotive, medical device production, and aerospace. Now ask yourself... *If we weren't smart people, would aerospace be one of our growing industries?*

We are intelligent Rednecks!

Rednecks now span across the United States because of the need for families to move and plant themselves where their work and trades are plentiful. It is no longer just the traditions of coal miners, mountain men, or country folk; it is one big ole melting pot with a lot of "roots."

13

THE MOST FAMOUS SAYIN'S

HEY YA'LL
BYE YA'LL

HEY Y'ALL

BYE Y'ALL

BIOGRAPHY

Abigail Turner (Abby) was born in Western Nebraska, but her early childhood occurred growing up in Colorado. Her family had a plumbing and custom home-building business and traveled where the work was plentiful. The experiences of living in six different states allowed Abigail to adapt to various environments and enjoy new people.

Although having three older brothers helped open her eyes to the outdoors and adjust to understanding males, she still loved "girly things." Then, her younger sister Rachel came along. It was a new world for Abby, and her faith in God was strengthened as she had her entire class praying that the baby would be a girl. The family was complete.

Abigail has dedicated herself to helping others make a positive difference within their circumstances. She has always encouraged students and adults to aspire, believe in, and develop their gifts and talents. Her parents and teachers instilled these values in her from a young age, and they continue to be a cornerstone in her life.

In the sixth grade, Abby began her entrepreneurial side. From lucrative lemonade stands and selling hand-made bracelets to teaching private flute lessons to high schoolers, she loved the thrill of the chase and following dreams. The light had been lit!

During college, she pivoted from her flute professor's encouragement to perform full-time. Upon graduating from the University of Wyoming with a bachelor's in music education, Abby knew that helping others was primary and that she would pour herself into the art of music *and* people. She has developed numerous music programs for schools and has a variety of professional groups that she has performed with for over three decades with her primary instrument, the flute.

The collection of her experiences and attention to fine detail has contributed to her propensity to help authors and musicians create foundations for their literary works and expand their artistic expressions.

The last of the six states that Abby has lived in is Alabama, the beautiful. The exquisite panorama of its forestry and landscapes has deepened her love of nature and an appreciation of its people. It is truly Sweet Home Alabama for Abby. She and her husband, David, live in a small rural area in L.A. (Lower Alabama).

Abigail and her mother founded their publishing company in 2018, PipStones Publishing (PipStones, LLC).

facebook.com/pipstonespublishing

x.com/pip_stones

instagram.com/pipstones

tiktok.com/pipstonespublishing

youtube.com/pipstonespublishing8802

PipStones

"Weavers of Tales and Tellers of Truth"

PipStones Publishing

MISSION STATEMENT:

Our mission is to publish unique and refreshing works from various authors and genres; to present and highlight literary endeavors in an ever-changing marketplace.

SERVICES:

Editing, Formatting, Illustrations, Publishing,

Distribution, Local & Social Marketing,

Basic Social Media Training/Set-Up

NOTE TO AN AUTHOR:

Reach out to us for a free author consultation and follow our social media for more book news and information!

(334)542-9271

https://www.pipstones.com

Eskimo Joe (A Musical Journey) *by Abigail Turner:*
Hardback Children's Book

Eskimo Joe (A Musical Journey) is a fusion of fun and learning for the family or classroom. Trek to rhythm and rhyme with Joe through a chalk pastel panorama of Alaska. Be sure to bundle this book with its classroom and homeschooling resource guide and downloadable narrated music.

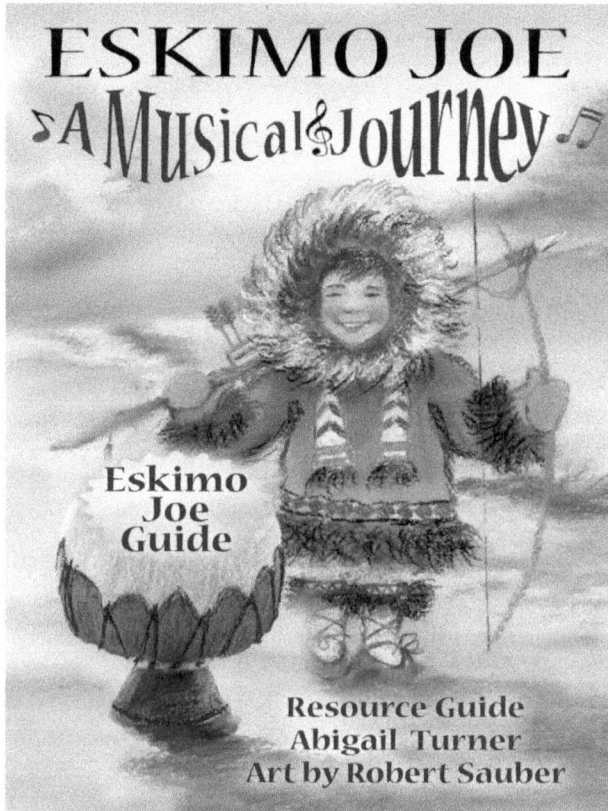

ESKIMO JOE
A Musical Journey

Eskimo
Joe
Guide

Resource Guide
Abigail Turner
Art by Robert Sauber

Eskimo Joe (**Resources Guide**): *Spiral-Bound Classroom Book*

Bundle this with the hardback book for fun, educational, and interesting additions to your classroom. Don't forget to go to our website and download the FREE narrated musical audio to accompany the books!

https://www.pipstones.com/eskimojoe

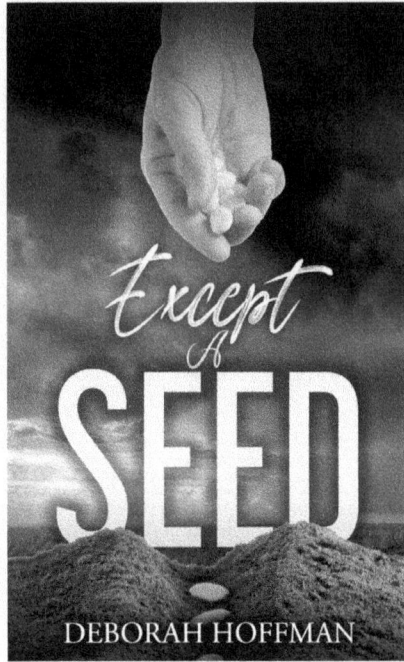

Except A Seed *by Deborah Hoffman: Christian Mystery Novel*

The death of a young college student precipitates a quest for truth and the eradication of an insidious evil. This is an intriguing revelation full of twists and turns.

Except A Seed on Amazon

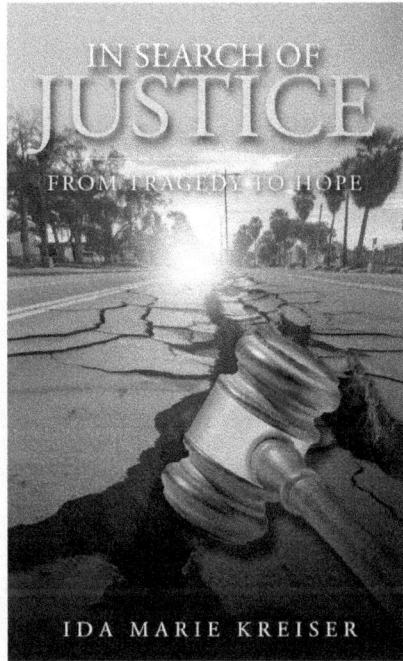

In Search of Justice, From Tragedy To Hope *by Ida Marie Kreiser: Memoir & Self-Help Book*

A true story of a mother who refuses to give in to the injustice surrounding the violent death of her son. This read is an open-hearted baring of the soul to help others break the bondage of devastating grief and rage.

In Search of Justice on Amazon

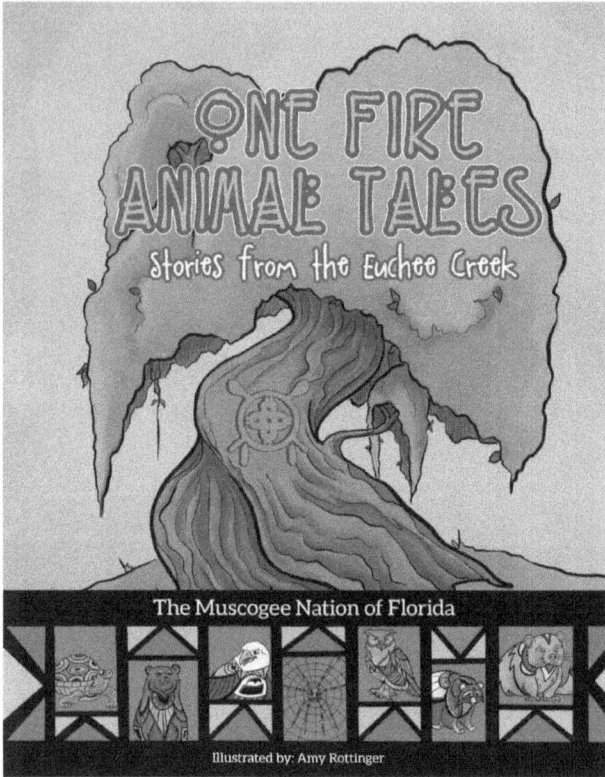

One Fire Animal Tales *by the Muscogee Nation of Florida: Children's Book*

This book encompasses the rich heritage and language of the people of one fire (The Euchee Creek). This written treasury preserves the oral ancient tales passed down through time. As you turn the pages, prepare to view the captivating art and the legends of The One Above, The Master of Breath, and the things He created.

One Fire Animal Tales on Amazon

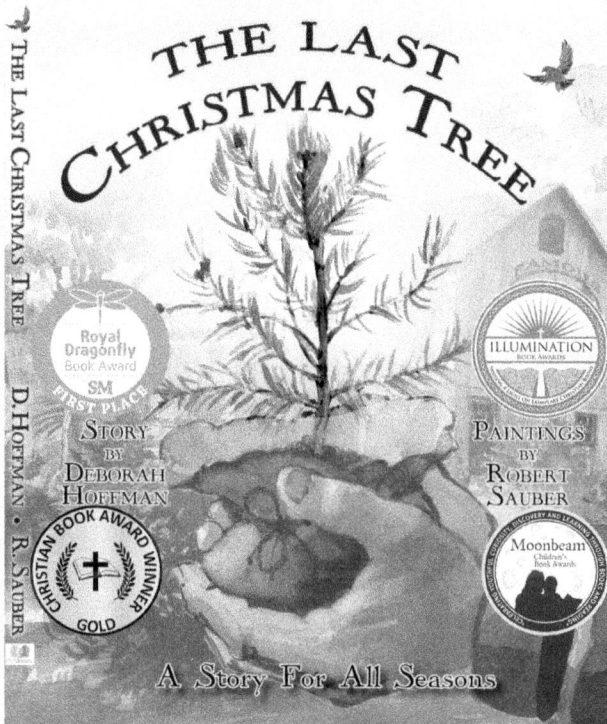

The Last Christmas Tree *by Deborah Hoffman*

The Last Christmas Tree is a treasured family gift book about a little tree named Twig, a farmer named Mr. B., and the One who is the maker of ALL things. This beautifully illustrated book imparts a lasting message for all ages and seasons.

Awards:

Gold— Christian Book Awards (Picture Book)

Gold— Royal Dragonfly Book Awards (Children's Picture Book)

Silver— Royal Dragonfly Book Awards (Best Illustrations)

Gold— Illumination Awards (Holiday Book)

Bronze— Moonbeam Book Awards (Children's Picture Book)

Honorable Mention— Readers' Favorite Awards (Picture Book)

The Last Christmas Tree also received Five-Star Editorial Reviews from Kirkus, Readers' Favorite, and Christian Book Award.

Go to: www.pipstones.com for more information.

The Last Christmas Tree on Amazon

or at www.pipstones.com

THANK YOU FOR READING *REDNECK SAYIN'S & TERMS!*

BYE YA'LL!

www.ingramcontent.com/pod-product-compliance
Lightning Source LLC
Chambersburg PA
CBHW052024030426
42335CB00026B/3274